Contents

What is Rock Climbing?

Imagine this: the sun warms your back, and a light wind keeps you cool. But your arms and legs are straining, because they're keeping you standing on a tiny ledge, facing a rock face. And you're 30 metres above a hard landing! Sound good? Then read on.

The First Climbers

Rock climbing first became popular in the 1800s. Daredevil mountain explorers began trying to climb the steepest slopes, where walking was impossible. They climbed in heavy hobnailed boots. For safety, they threaded a rope into a crack in the rock, and bashed pebbles in to keep the rope in place. If they fell, and the pebbles held, the rope would stop them from splatting on the ground below.

These young climbers are taking their first steps in the sport. Who knows if one of them might one day be winning climbing competitions?

Climbing Today

Today, climbers have much better safety equipment than in the past. This means they are able to tackle increasingly tricky climbs. Some of today's top climbers use handholds so tiny, they are hard to see. Even with modern safety gear, though, climbing is still dangerous. Every year, many climbers are badly injured or even killed in falls.

Climbing Indoors

Today, many people practise their climbing techniques on indoor climbing walls in sports centres. These walls use artificial holds that are designed to feel like rock. The holds can be moved around to make the wall harder or easier to climb, depending on who is using it. Indoor walls are very safe, and also allow climbers to practise in the warm and dry, even in winter.

Indoor climbing walls such as this one are increasingly popular. They can be used by climbers of any ability, from beginner to expert.

Getting Started

If you want to give climbing a try, the best place to start is at your local climbing wall. Many sports centres have climbing walls: telephone round to find one, or you could try an Internet search (see page 29).

The Belayer

The belayer stands close to the bottom of the climb, looking up. He or she takes in the rope as the climber gets higher up. The rope must never have any slack in it, but should also not be too tight, as this can pull the climber off balance.

Introductory Sessions

Many climbing wall centres run introductory sessions. These are a good way to find out if you enjoy climbing. The centres provide safety equipment such as helmets and harnesses. They may even loan out extra-sticky rock-climbing shoes. Experienced teachers supervise and make sure no one is injured.

Top Roping

Most people's first climb is 'top roped'. In top roping, the rope is tied to your safety harness. Then it stretches up above you to the top of the climb, through a ring or anchor point, and back down to the ground. A belayer holds the other end of the rope, gathering it in as the climber goes up. If the climber slips, the belayer grips the rope tight and stops the climber from falling.

A climber ascends a rope, while a belayer assists at the bottom.

This is a belay device, which the belayer uses to hold the rope securely if the climber falls. There are several different kinds of belay device.

Basic Technique

The key to good climbing technique is to use as little energy as possible. Leg muscles are stronger than arms and shoulders, so it is better to climb by stepping up to new footholds than by hauling yourself up using your arms.

DON'T! Stretch for holds like this climber unless you really have to. A long reach like this uses a lot of energy, and is more likely to throw the climber off balance.

DO! Try to make short movements. Small steps up and short reaches with your arms use little energy and are less likely to affect your balance.

Dos and Don'ts

DON'T! Hug the rock face like this. It is not good technique, because your arms and shoulders are taking a lot of your weight.

DO! Keep your legs and body fairly straight and lean away from the wall slightly. This way, the strong muscles of your legs take most of the weight.

Basic Equipment

Climbing does not have to be expensive. When you first start climbing, there are only a few bits of equipment you really need. It is a good idea to buy most things new, but some can even be bought second-hand.

Personal Equipment

For top roping, a climber only needs a few basic pieces of personal equipment:

- Most important is a harness, which goes around a climber's waist and legs. The rope and other safety gear are attached to the harness, so it is vital that this fits well and is in good condition.
- Climbers usually also wear a helmet, for safety.
- Climbing shoes that give extra grip are needed on all but the simplest routes.
- A screw-shut karabiner (see page 11) is used to attach the rope to your harness.

General Equipment

Climbers need a few pieces of general equipment to go top roping. Often a group of friends club together and share the cost of these:

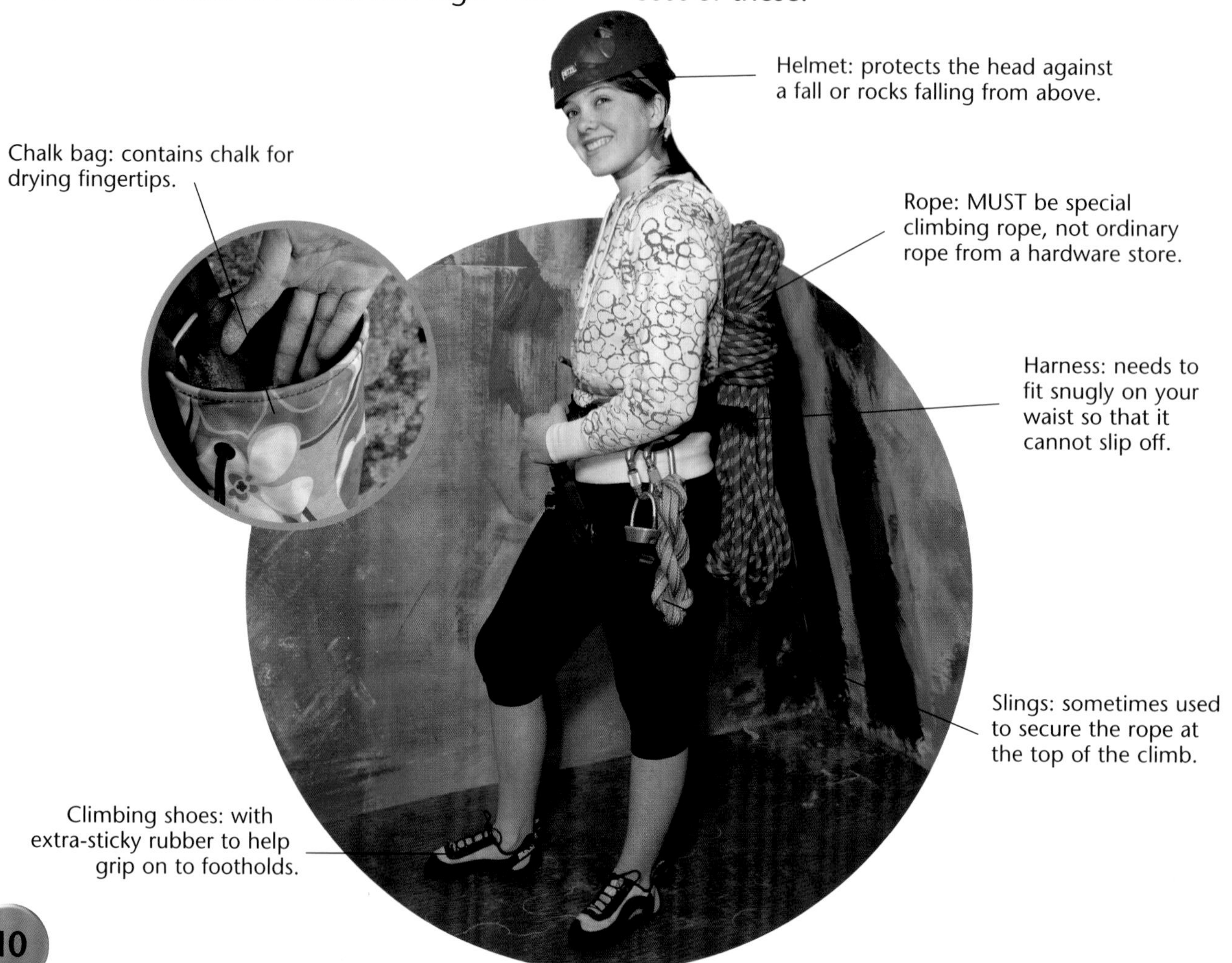

Helmet: protects the head against a fall or rocks falling from above.

Chalk bag: contains chalk for drying fingertips.

Rope: MUST be special climbing rope, not ordinary rope from a hardware store.

Harness: needs to fit snugly on your waist so that it cannot slip off.

Slings: sometimes used to secure the rope at the top of the climb.

Climbing shoes: with extra-sticky rubber to help grip on to footholds.

- Rope. NEVER buy a second-hand rope. Climbing ropes can only take the weight of a set number of falls before they need to be replaced, and you will not know how many a second-hand rope has had.
- Slings and screw-shut karabiners, for anchoring the rope at the top of the climb.

Joining a Climbing Club

One good way to get into climbing is to join a club. Clubs often organise climbing trips, and may even be able to lend you some equipment until you get your own. The other members will give you advice and encouragement, too. Staff at your local climbing wall may be able to help you find a club.

Screw-shut karabiners are important basic kit.

This climber prefers the feel of slightly looser clothes. If you wear loose clothes like these, it is important to be sure that they cannot get caught up in your climbing gear.

This climber has chosen to wear tighter-fitting clothes. It is important that the clothing is stretchy, so that it doesn't stop her stretching for holds.

Climbing Knots

If there is one thing every climber needs to know, it is how to tie knots well. Getting a knot wrong can have disastrous results. Imagine leaning back on the rope halfway up a climb, only to feel the knot you tied in it unravelling!

End-of-Rope Knots

Knots at the end of a rope are used in every climb. The climber has to make a loop at the end of the rope to attach it to his or her harness. Most climbers use a figure-8 knot for this. In fact, this knot is so useful that some climbers get through their whole climbing career only knowing the two versions on the figure-8.

Figure-8 Knot

1 *Hold the rope with about two metres spare at the end. Turn it back on itself and over, creating a loop.*

2 *Tuck the rope under itself, then pass it down through the loop. Do not pull the knot tight!*

3 *Pass the end through whatever it is being tied to, then tuck the rope back through the knot, following the rope's path in reverse.*

4 *Pull the knot tight.*

This version of the figure-8 knot is called the figure-8 loop. It is tied using a double length of rope. This means it can be used to add a loop to the middle of a climbing rope, as well as to the ends.

Loop Knots

Loop knots are used to make a loop in the middle of the rope. They are often used on multi-pitch routes, as a way of attaching one of the climbers to a safe belay point. The figure-8 loop can be used, but the alpine butterfly is just as quick to tie and stronger.

Linking Ropes and Tapes

Sometimes climbers need to link two ropes together. To do this, they make a simple loop in the end of one rope and pass the end through the loop. Then they take the end of the other rope, and follow this route backwards, so that the two ropes snake through side by side, with a long tag at each side. Pulling these tight links the ropes.

Alpine Butterfly Knot

1 *Give the rope two twists, making an '8' shape from two loops.*

2 *Drop the top loop down and over the rope.*

3 *Pull it up through the bottom loop on the other side.*

4 *Pull on the end of the loop until the knot tightens.*

Natural Rock

After learning the ropes on an indoor wall, most climbers start climbing outdoors. Climbing outdoors on natural rock is different from climbing indoors. The rock can be slippery, and the holds sometimes break off. For safety, most climbers start outdoors with top ropes.

Secure Anchor Points

When top-roping outdoors, it is crucial to find a secure anchor point for the rope. Some specialist climbing centres install these for climbers, but in other places you have to find an anchor point of your own. A rock-solid tree often makes a good anchor, or perhaps a giant, immovable rock. Experienced climbers use two anchor points unless they are 100% sure one is safe.

The **WRONG** way to fix a top rope. The sling is too short, so the karabiner does not hang over the top edge of the climb. When the rope is pulled in by the belayer, it will rub on the rock, and could be damaged or broken.

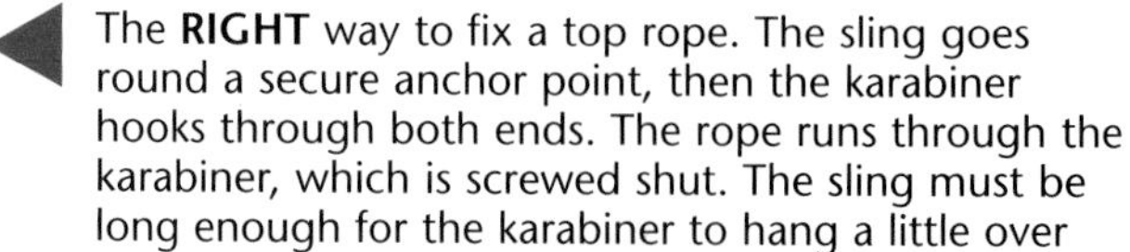

The **RIGHT** way to fix a top rope. The sling goes round a secure anchor point, then the karabiner hooks through both ends. The rope runs through the karabiner, which is screwed shut. The sling must be long enough for the karabiner to hang a little over the top edge of the climb.

The end of the rope is attached to the climber's harness using a figure-8 knot (see page 12) and a screw-gate karabiner.

The other end of the rope goes through a belay device, which is attached to the belayer's harness using a screw-gate karabiner. The belayer then takes in the slack, and everything is ready for the climber to start.

Safety

Once the anchor point is fixed and both ends of the rope are dangling down from it, the climber ties on to one end. The belayer pulls the rope taut and attaches his or her belay device. For safety, the climber and the belayer check that each other's harnesses are done up properly, and that the knots and karabiners linking them to the rope are also secure.

Testing the Rock

Natural rock can sometimes break off when someone's weight goes on to it. Climbers test whether this might happen by trying a hold before putting their full weight on it. If the rock is wobbly or creaky, they use a different hold!

As the climber goes up, the belayer takes in rope through the belay device.

Bouldering

Today, a type of climbing called bouldering is becoming increasingly popular. In bouldering, climbers avoid climbing high up. Instead, they try to find tricky or interesting climbing problems near to the ground, where they are less likely to be seriously hurt if they fall.

Bouldering Equipment

Because bouldering is done at low level, the climbers do not use ropes and harnesses. They have just sticky rock shoes, and a chalk bag on a string around their waist. Carrying less gear means they are holding a little less weight, and can try even trickier moves than usual.

The other piece of bouldering equipment is a bouldering mat. This is a padded mat laid down under the boulder. It absorbs some of the force of a fall if the climber slips.

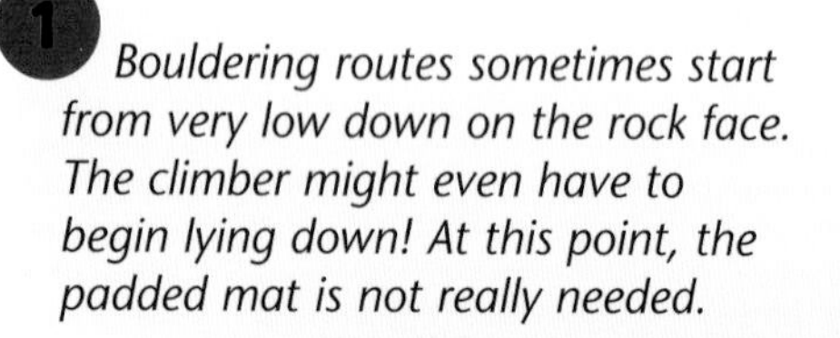

1 *Bouldering routes sometimes start from very low down on the rock face. The climber might even have to begin lying down! At this point, the padded mat is not really needed.*

Indoor Bouldering

2 *As the climber gets higher, the spotter moves in underneath her. The spotter watches the climber carefully, and gives advice about how to do the climb. The spotter also makes sure the mat stays underneath the climber.*

Bouldering Locations

Once you know where to look, there are places to go bouldering everywhere. People practise their bouldering by climbing along walls, in indoor and outdoor climbing centres, at the base of cliffs, and – of course – on big boulders. Just make sure before you start that bouldering is allowed!

Chris Sharma (USA) swings by one hand at the top of the wall in the men's rock climbing final during the Gorge Games. Sharma won the event.

3 *If the climber does fall, the spotter can sometimes help. She tries to take some of the force of the fall, usually by catching the climber under the armpits. Of course, the spotter has to make sure she's not injured herself.*

Chris Sharma

Date of Birth: April 23rd, 1981

Nationality: American

Chris Sharma is a professional rock climber. He first burst onto the rock-climbing scene at the age of just 14, when he won the US national bouldering championship. Climbs are divided into grades depending on their technical difficulty and the degree of risk involved in the climb. At 15 Sharma was climbing at a grade that is so difficult, only a handful of climbers ever reach it.

Among his other achievements:

- **In 2001, climbing the *Realization* route in France.**
- **Completing several other routes which are so difficult, no one else can do them!**
- **Being the first to climb probably the world's hardest boulder problem, 'Witness the Fitness' in the United States.**

Adventure and Sport Climbing

Once they have got some experience of outdoor climbing, most climbers start to climb without a rope stretching above them. Instead, a lead climber trails the rope behind, attaching it to the rock for safety. The second climber follows, unclipping the rope as he or she climbs.

Further to Fall

Climbing without the rope above you is more dangerous than top roping (which is probably what makes it more exciting!). The lead climber is nearly always above the place where the rope is attached to the rock. If the lead climber falls, he or she falls down past the attachment point, then the same distance again, before the rope takes his or her weight.

This pair of climbers are ready to set off. Each has one end of the rope attached to her harness. The second climber, or second, also holds the rope in a belay device. The second will use this to hold the lead climber, or leader, if she falls.

As the leader climbs up, the second pays the rope out. She makes sure the rope is loose, so that it does not pull the leader off. But it must not be too loose, or the rope won't stop the leader quickly enough if she slips.

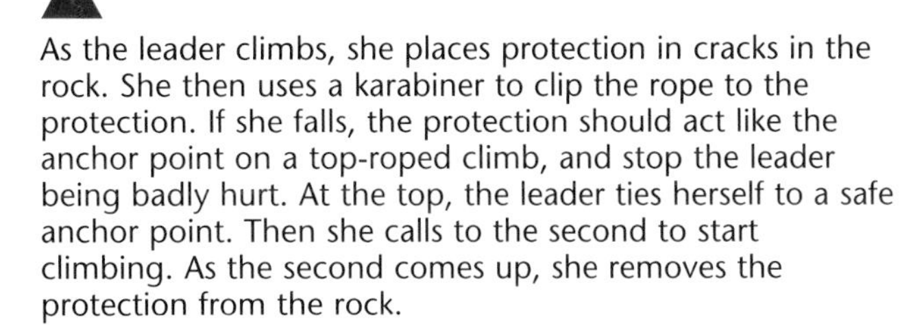

As the leader climbs, she places protection in cracks in the rock. She then uses a karabiner to clip the rope to the protection. If she falls, the protection should act like the anchor point on a top-roped climb, and stop the leader being badly hurt. At the top, the leader ties herself to a safe anchor point. Then she calls to the second to start climbing. As the second comes up, she removes the protection from the rock.

A range of protection devices clipped to a climber's belt. Climbers call this a 'rack'.

Adventure Climbing

In adventure climbing, the lead climber attaches the rope to the rock using protection devices (see above). There are many different kinds of protection, but almost all work by being jammed into a crack in the rock. The danger is that climbers don't know for certain if the protection will stay in place until they fall!

Sport Climbing

Sport climbers do not carry protection devices with them. Instead, they attach the rope to bolts – rings that have been permanently attached to the rock face. Sport climbing is safer than adventure climbing.

On sport routes the rope is clipped to bolts like this, rather than to protection.

Working as a Team

Climbers on 'lead' routes need to work together as a team. They have to be able to let each other know what is happening – even when they cannot see or hear one another.

Making Safe

When the leader finishes a climb, he or she 'makes safe'. This means tying his or her harness securely to the rock, so that it would be impossible to fall down. Now the leader will be able to hold the second climber safely on the rope if he or she slips on the way up.

Leader and Second

1 *The leader has 'made safe', and calls down to the second. Many people shout, 'SAFE!', or if they cannot hear each other, tug on the rope twice. The second shouts back, 'OK!' and takes the rope out of the belay device.*

2 *The leader takes in all the slack in the rope, then attaches it to her belay device and shouts down: 'ON BELAY!' Once the second is ready to start climbing, she shouts: 'CLIMBING!' The leader shouts, 'OK!' and takes in the rope as the second climbs up.*

Bringing up the Second

Once the leader has made safe, the second climber can start up the route. The leader pulls in the rope as the second comes up. For the second, the climb is almost as safe as if he or she were top-roped. The rope stretches up above. It's only possible to fall if the leader has not made safe properly.

Multi-Pitch Routes

Some climbs are more than one rope-length in height. This means the climbers have to stop at a belay. The second climber comes up and makes safe, then the first climber sets off for the top again.

Lynn Hill heads for a monster roof problem on the route known as 'Burning' – probably because of the burning pain it gives your arms.

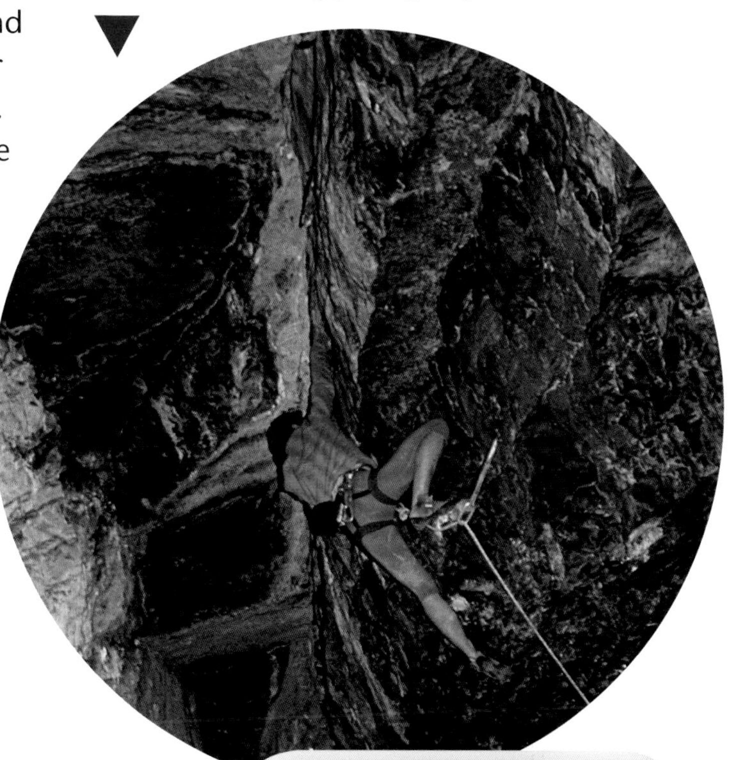

With the rope stretching above, the second does not need the protection. She removes it from the rock and clips it to her harness.

Lynn Hill

Born: 1961

Nationality: American

Lynn Hill is a groundbreaking female climber. In 1993 she became the first person ever to climb The Nose route in Yosemite Valley 'free' – i.e. without any artificial aids. A year later she repeated the climb solo, in under 24 hours. It was over 10 years before anyone else managed to repeat these amazing climbs.

Among Hill's other achievements:

- **In 1979, she became the first woman ever to climb Ophir Broke in Colorado, USA, one of the most difficult climbs in the world.**
- **In 1991, Hill again set a new standard for women's climbing when she climbed Masse Critique in France.**

Developing Technique

Once you start to climb harder routes, you need to develop new techniques. Some of these seem like magic! They allow you to gain a grip with your hands and feet where previously you wouldn't have been able to see a hold.

Three Contact Points

Contact points are the parts of your body which are touching the rock as you climb. There are four: two hands and two feet. One of the basic rules of climbing technique is to keep three contact points with the rock at all times. From beginner to expert, all good climbers keep this rule in mind.

Climbing across a roof, hanging upside down, seems like it should be impossible. For experienced climbers, though, good technique allows them to zip across the roof like a bat!

Contact Points

1 *As the climber approaches the roof section, his feet are still on the vertical face. Gravity pushes most of his weight down through his feet.*

2 *Once the climber is on the roof, he keeps at least three contact points with the rock the whole time. His hands and feet push away from his body, which acts like a spring holding a shower rail in place between two walls.*

Fancy Footwork

Footwork (where and how you position your feet while climbing) is probably the most important technique to develop. Many beginners feel safest hugging themselves against the rock face, which puts too much weight on their arms.

Experienced climbers learn to trust their super-sticky shoes. These will grip the rock incredibly well if they have the climber's weight pushing down on them. To achieve this, climbers angle their heels outwards and point their toes straight at the rock face as much as possible (see bottom right photo). This concentrates a lot of their weight on to a small area, making the shoe grip the rock as well as possible.

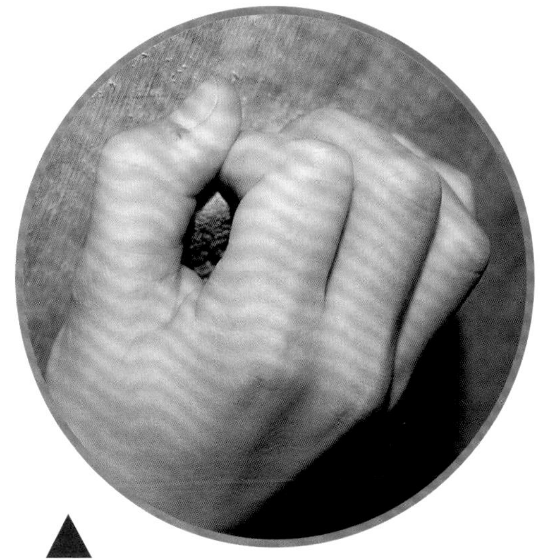

'Crimping', or folding your thumb and fingers together like this, is a way to get a grip on the tiniest handholds.

3 *As the climber leaves the roof, he keeps at least one foot in contact with the rock while the other one swings up and onto the vertical face. Otherwise he will swing out and take all his weight on his arms and shoulders.*

This is good footwork. The climber has his heel pointing outwards, which will hold his body away from the rock. This puts more weight into his feet and less into his arms.

Abseiling

Once you're up, you have to come down. Some routes you can walk down from, but others are so inaccessible that there's no way out! This is where abseiling – or sliding down a rope – comes in.

Setting up an Anchor

The moment when climbers put all their weight into the rope over a steep drop is pretty terrifying! They need to be 100% sure that the rope is attached to a secure anchor point. Most climbers use two anchor points, connected to the rope with slings. That way, their weight is not all concentrated into one place.

Using two anchor points instead of one means the weight of the abseiler is shared out. Also, if one of the anchors fails, the other should still hold the climber.

Sliding Down

To slide down an anchored rope, climbers use an abseil device. The rope is passed through the device, which is attached to the climber's harness. There are several different kinds, but they all work in a similar way.

As the rope slides through, it is slowed down by the way it rubs against the abseil device. The angle at which the climber holds the rope decides how fast he or she slides down it. The climber can slide down fast, slowly, or even stop completely.

Experienced climbers always double-check that their harness is done up securely before abseiling.

With the 'downhill' rope (the loose end, which dangles down to the ground) at any less than 90° to the 'uphill' rope, climbers will slide downwards. The smaller the angle, the faster they will slide.

If the climber moves the downhill rope backwards, towards her body, she slides down the rope more slowly. With the rope at this angle, the climber has stopped sliding completely.

Body Position

Climbers aim to keep their bodies angled at 90° to the slope as they abseil down. This keeps them away from the rock, and allows them to push away from obstacles.

Abseil Checklist

All careful climbers (and most of the careless ones are dead) run through a checklist before they abseil down a rope.

They double-check that:

- the anchor points are secure
- the rope is in good condition and properly attached to the anchor
- their harness is done up
- the belay device is securely attached to their harness.

If they have any doubts about the answers, experienced climbers do not abseil.

Competition Climbing

Climbers have always competed with each other. Every climber wants to be able to climb harder routes than his or her friends, or to be able to do more difficult boulder problems. But from the late 1980s onwards, climbers began gathering for official contests.

Contest Format

Contests are usually held on an artificial climbing wall, often an indoor wall. There are categories for leading, bouldering and speed climbing. The route is set at a certain level of difficulty, and the climbers are only allowed to use the holds that are part of the route. They must clip the rope to bolts on the wall as they go up. The climbers who get highest go through to the next round, in which they all climb a new route.

The Isolation Room

Before they compete, the climbers are usually kept in an isolation room. They are not allowed to see the route until it is their turn to climb. Once they come out of the room, they have a set amount of time to study the route, then they must begin climbing.

A climber in the isolation room preparing to go out and compete. To make the contest equal, none of the climbers is allowed to see the route before they climb it.

Studying the route before you start, and working out the order in which to use the holds that best suits your climbing style, is a bit like working out a jigsaw puzzle.

Having worked out the route, the climber begins. He will aim to climb quickly but smoothly, saving as much strength as possible for the trickiest moves. At places on the route there will be big holds, which climbers call jugs, where they can get a rest.

Scoring

In lead climbing, the climbers are allowed a set time on the route (usually between six and eight minutes). Once the time is up, they are scored according to how far they got. Each hold on the contest route is given a score number – for example, 20. To get that score, the climber must touch the hold. If he or she then falls off, a score of 20 is given. If the climber reaches the hold and then falls off going for the next one, he or she scores 20+. In a close contest, 20+ would beat 20.

In speed climbing, the fastest climber to complete a route up a 15-metre high wall is the winner.

Statistics and Records

2008 European Champions

Men, lead climbing: Patxi Usobiaga Lakunza (Spain)
Women, lead climbing: Johanna Ernst (Austria)
Men, bouldering: Jérome Meyer (France)
Women, bouldering: Natalija Gros (Slovenia)

2008 Asian Champions

Men, lead climbing: Sachi Anma (Japan)
Women, lead climbing: Ja In Kim (Korea)
Men, bouldering: Tsukuru Hori (Japan)
Women, bouldering: Ja In Kim (Korea)
Men, speed: Qixin Jhong (China)
Women, speed: Cuifang He (China)

2007 World Champions

Men, lead climbing: Ramon Julian Puigblanque (Spain)
Women, lead climbing: Angela Eiter (Austria)
Men, bouldering: Dmitry Sarafutdinov (Russia)
Women, bouldering: Anna Stohr (Austria)
Men, speed: Qixin Jhong (China)
Women, speed: Tatiana Ruyga (Russia)
Men, combined disciplines: Dmitry Sarafutdinov (Russia)
Women, combined disciplines: Jenny Lavarda (Italy)

Speed climbing world records

Men's
15 Metre Speed World Record: Qixin Zhong, 7.35
(2008 World Cup Finals in Qinghai, China)

Women's
15 Metre Speed World Record: Li Chun Hua, 10.58
(2008 World Cup semi-finals in Qinghai, China)

Glossary

Anchor point A place to which a climbing rope can safely be attached.

Belayer The person holding the rope in a belay device, ready to stop a climber's fall.

Bolts Rings that have been permanently attached to the rock face.

Creaky A word climbers use to describe a handhold or foothold that seems loose.

First ascent A climb that is done for the first time.

Handholds Places where a climber will be able to hold on with his or her hands.

Hobnailed Describing a boot that has nails banged into the sole.

Karabiner A loop of metal with a hinge that can be opened or closed.

Leader One of a pair or group of climbers who goes up first.

Problems The name climbers give to tricky moves.

Protection A device or devices attached to the rock face, to which a rope can be attached.

Roof climb A climb that crosses an upside-down space.

Routes Specific climbs, or ways up a steep slope.

Second The climber who comes up after the leader.

Slack Looseness in the rope.

Slings Loops of strong tape or rope.

Takes in Gathers in rope until it is taut.

Ties on Attaches the rope, usually to a harness or an anchor point.

Websites

www.climbing.com
The website of the British magazine *Climbing*, this is an excellent place to keep up with news about climbing in the UK and Europe. The site deals with mountaineering as well as rock climbing.

www.ifsc-climbing.org
Home page of the International Federation of Sport Climbing, this is the place to find out about the results of recent climbing contests.

www.rockclimbing.com
A good site with all kinds of information about the climbing scene, from routes and equipment to a lively forum.

www.thebmc.co.uk
Home page of the British Mountaineering Council: click on 'Climbing walls', then 'Find a wall' for help finding a climbing centre near where you live. The site can also help you find a climbing club.

Note to parents and teachers: every effort has been made by the Publishers to ensure that these websites are suitable for children, that they are of the highest educational value, and that they contain no inappropriate or offensive material. However, because of the nature of the Internet, it is impossible to guarantee that the contents of these sites will not be altered. We strongly advise that Internet access is supervised by a responsible adult.

Index

KNOW YOUR SPORT

Rock Climbing

Yvonne Thorpe

W

First published in 2009 by
Franklin Watts
338 Euston Road
London NW1 3BH

Franklin Watts Australia
Level 17/207 Kent Street
Sydney NSW 2000

Series editor: Jeremy Smith
Art director: Jonathan Hair

Series designed and created for
Franklin Watts by Storeybooks.
Designer: Rita Storey
Editor: Nicola Edwards
Photography: Jon Hare
www.fullfatphotography.com

A CIP catalogue record for this book
is available from the British Library.

Dewey classification: 796.52'23
ISBN 978 0 7496 8860 8

Printed in China

Note: At the time of going to press, the statistics in this book were up to date. However, it is possible because of the climbers' ongoing participation in the sport that some of these may now be out of date.

Picture credits
© Troy Wayrynen/NewSport/Corbis p17,
© Galen Rowell/CORBIS p21.

Cover images: Jon Hare

All photos posed by models.
Thanks to Elaine Budden, Kelly Budden,
Robi Kerr and Jack Luckhurst.

The Publisher would like to thank everyone at The Barn Climbing Centre (www.barn-climbing.co.uk) Devon for all their help.

WARNING
This book is not a substitute for learning from a skilled coach, which is the only safe way to learn climbing techniques.